STL
Scavenger

Dea Hoover

Library of Congress Control Number: 2020950502

ISBN: 9781681063102

Cover and interior design by Claire Ford

Cover and interior photos by Cory Weaver Photography, Dea Hoover, and Don Korte. Clip art courtesy of Pixabay and Wikimedia Commons.

Printed in the United States of America
21 22 23 24 25   5 4 3 2 1

Dedication

To my husband Declan, co-conspirator in rhyme, and true companion in love and life.

To Mom, who started my love of reading and hence writing. She taught me to finish what I start.

To Dad, you live through me giving me courage and the love of relentless pursuit. We miss you!

Contents

Acknowledgments

When Nancy Milton introduced me to Josh Stevens at Reedy Press via email in 2019, I never dreamed our meeting at Chris' Pancake & Dining would lead to my first book. Thanks to my faithful office manager, tour coordinator, and friend Maggie Rutherford; my supportive husband, business partner, and rhyming consultant Declan Rutan; and our parents, Donna Hoover, Bob Rutan, and Kathy Rutan, who pushed me forward, asking, "How's the book going?"

Meeting the challenge required help from the following people including: Barb Northcott without whom I'd be a rudderless ship during this process; Taree McGee, Julie Nicolai, and Dennis Maag for providing photos at the last moment; Kelly Mazzacavallo for connecting me to Bryce Robinson; and University City Mayor Terry Crow, LaRette Reese, Winnie Sullivan, Carol Diaz-Granados, Meridith McKinley, Joe Edwards, Harry Weber, Sherry Sissack, Lynda Hofstetter, Jason Gray, Dana Gray, Greg Maxon, Shannon Sowell, Wiktor Szostalo, Pete Manzo, LynnMarie Alexander, Monsignor Vincent Bommarito, AnnMarie Lumetta, Alderman Joe Vollmer, and Amy De La Hunt.

Introduction

My life in St. Louis began as a wide-eyed freshman at a local university. Previously, St. Louis was where I had visited from Vandalia, Missouri, going to the Saint Louis Zoo, Six Flags Over Mid-America, the Gateway Arch, and even a baseball game at Busch Stadium. Upon arrival I learned people lived in neighborhoods that resembled my small town. I discovered tasty delights such as frozen custard, toasted ravioli, and gooey butter cake.

I was hooked! I've lived here for the past three decades and savored every moment.

When the idea of a scavenger hunt book encompassing the metro area's neighborhoods and towns was presented, I thought it sounded a lot like what I do every day. I'm a local tour guide. People come with me looking to find the usual but most importantly, the unusual places and locations in the area. I choose the routes because they are interesting to me. From international guests traveling Route 66 to student groups in performance competition to parents of prospective college students, I find that everyone is interested in why and how buildings and places came to be in St. Louis and around the area. I also believe my general sense of curiosity is a great asset to my job—it sure helped me when creating this adventure!

Inside you will find at least 20 photographs per neighborhood or town. Each photo has a short hint as to where it is and what it is. In this modern age of technology I fully expect phones will be employed to help the seeker find the way. Once the site has been spotted, my desire is that more information will be sought to understand why I chose that particular location or object.

I hope you pick up this book with unfettered enthusiasm for learning about St. Louis. Whether this is your first visit or you are a native, as 69 percent of St. Louisans are, this book may lead you to locations you never knew existed nor expected to find. The older areas have experienced a renaissance with many new facets to discover. Newer areas are growing and developing their own sense of style. Be sure to stop in the local shops, restaurants, cafés, and bookstores along the way and get to know the area you covered. One section at a time, I hope you take in the beauty, learn a bit of history, and most of all have fun, as you search for each answer.

Ready, set, go!

 **St. Charles**

Florissant

I-70

I-270

Ferguson

I-70

University City

Clayton

Central West End

The Hill

I-64

I-44

Tower Grove South

Webster Groves

Kirkwood   **Southampton**

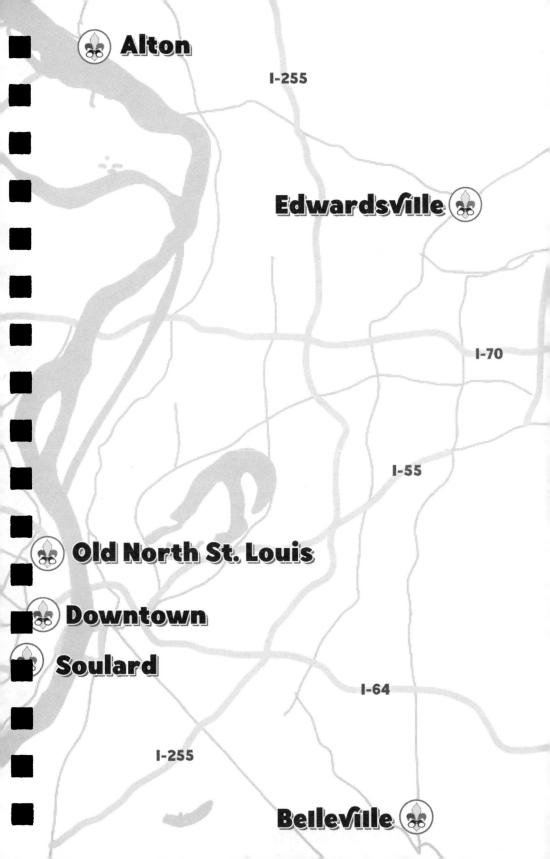

1

Come here to find pens that click
Paintbrushes that paint thin or thick.
The company started in Galesburg, Illinois
And many in town they do employ.

_____

_____

2

POWERFUL VOICE
RAW INTENSITY

Look down at the ground and you might
See what's up in the sky at night.
So many to search, but don't quit!
Ask, "What's love got to do with it?"

_____

_____

3

They say that you might find your thrill
At this hip music hotspot and grill.
You might get a little starstruck
In rooms named for a King or a Duck.

4

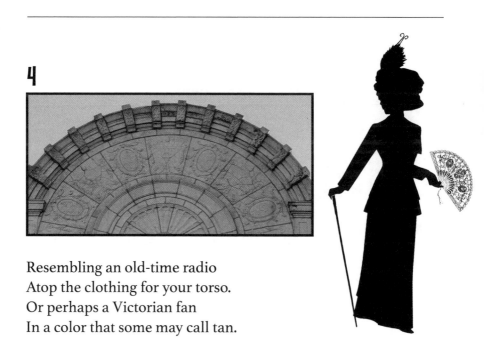

Resembling an old-time radio
Atop the clothing for your torso.
Or perhaps a Victorian fan
In a color that some may call tan.

5

A diamond design masonry
Tops this biz confectionary.
A first date you could meet
Sharing a soda sweet.

6

On this street's walk of fame find this statue
Of the guy who said, "Maybellene! Be true!"
He's busting his signature move
Encouraging fans to find their groove.

7

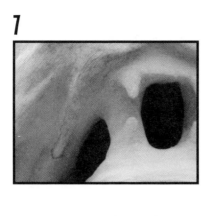

Have you seen the striking pair of cats?
Upon a pillar, 100 years they have sat.
Opportunity is what they stand for—
You can practically hear them roar!

8

Whether 'tis day or 'tis night
Spy this celestial satellite
Atop Joe's hotel the orb spins
Beckoning all to "C'mon in!"

9

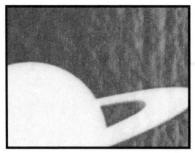

Look around as you start to stroll
You'll find yourself passing by Sol.
As you head through the walk of stars
Stop at the one that once made cars.

10

The first part of the name suggests wine
But it's circles of vinyl you'll find.
Seeking 33, 45, 78?
You're certain to find something great.

11

The facade is truly remarkable!
(The building is really octagonal.)
Built in '03 for *The Woman's Magazine*
Its 8-ton searchlight assures it will be seen.

12

Like reading that gets under the surface?
Stop in here for that very purpose.
They're specialists, and Indie's their angle,
Tough searches they're sure to untangle.

13

My mouth's watering . . . what's that smell?
Their fare will, for sure, ring your bell.
With lots of options, it's no pig in a poke—
Your tastebuds and appetite it will stoke.

14

The grande dame of the street's facade
Opened in '24—patrons were awed!
Brought back to grandeur in 1995
Helping art house filmmakers survive and thrive.

15

Straddling the demarcation
Of city and county separation.
A building named for the place
Where you can find its space.

_____

_____

16

"Hey Lenny! Hey Squiggy! Where's Laverne?"
This bottling machine's often whirrin'!
Packing St. Louis's cream pop
And beer sold at a soda shop.

_____

_____

17

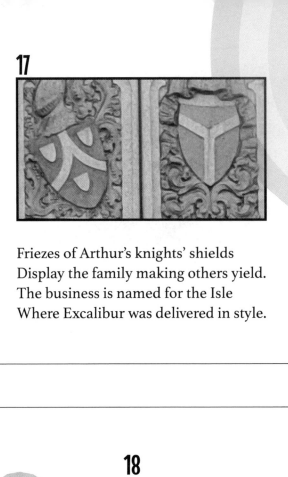

Friezes of Arthur's knights' shields
Display the family making others yield.
The business is named for the Isle
Where Excalibur was delivered in style.

18

A building between two stars
One was a poet of ours.
The other was our founding father
Neither's among us any longer.

19

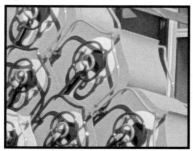

A strutter who fans his tail,
On all the decor, it prevails.
Neon beckons you in the door
For a burger, coffee, and more.

20

Below what looks like a flame
Your investment fears are tamed.
Just east of the entrance gates
Find this place offering rates.

21

What a wonderful campus park!
Even more if you're a Monarch.
Tiny visitors make your heart flutter
South of Forsyth, through a field of color.

22

Forget houses of straw or stick
This farmhouse is made out of brick.
The first of its kind in the West
It borders a Forever Forest.

1819

23

A wealthy businessman of local acclaim
Built these two elegant homes the same.
One of the homes is the Chancellor's place
You can dine at the other or rent out the space.

24

Walk along the street that means three,
Towering stonework you will see.
Near the place where young create
Hear the bells? You could be late!

1

The best players in the world have their name
Listed here, these masters of the game.
Twice the man outside held a record;
No one claims that his past was checkered.

_____

_____

2

After a long day (or long knight)
You might have worked up an appetite.
Named for the targeted man on the board
Offerings listed you can easily afford.

_____

_____

3

The game is easy to learn, this is true
But to get better takes time and a lesson or two.
You'll learn some new tricks to help you play faster.
Who knows? You might even meet a grand master!

_____

_____

4

This next clue, oh boy it's a doozy!
Outside of the building's a Newsy,
Inside there is much you can learn.
The only rule? If you borrow, please return.

_____

_____

5

If you live here you might think you're a bird
As the lines of art and architecture are blurred.
Looking like glass shards thrust into the ground—
If you're afraid of heights, don't look down!

6

She wrote of strong mothers and wives
With tales of their innermost lives.
Her stories still told, a century passed;
Her first home, St. Louis, was also her last.

7

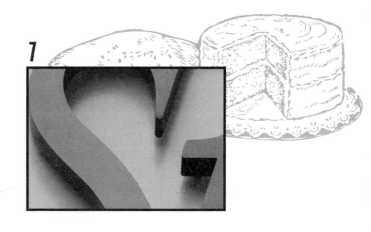

Perhaps not the largest, it's true
But it's known for the finest of food:
Prime cuts of meat and fresh seafood catch
Offering Miss Hulling's cakes from scratch!

_____

_____

8

A place to stay or catch a film at night
Head to the bar to enjoy the starlight.
Famous guests included both Frank and Dean—
It once was The Place to see and be seen!

_____

_____

9

Moved here to offer more access—
Sit here to relax and de-stress.
Found on the street named for our seventh state
Meet here before enjoying dining first-rate.

_____

_____

10

Founded by Wash U students in '69
If you like reading, this place is a shrine.
Browse the collection, with covers so pretty
Don't forget to lean down and pet the kitty!

_____

_____

11

Step 1, 2; turn 1, 2; twirl 1, 2; glide.
You'll learn to do more than just Electric Slide.
Hosts Michael and Ken warmly welcome you in
Visit once and you'll come back again and again.

12

"Let's meet for high tea!" to your friends you will say—
You'll feel you've discovered the Champs Élysées.
Dine in the lovely conservatory
And learn the namesake's enchanting life story.

13

Hey, wait just a minute! Where did the "e" go?
Here's a clue: it's the same as the area code.
This local place has a name that's irrational
But in recent years, they've expanded to national.

14

It's so big and historic, can't imagine the scope
Of this holy building, once blessed by the Pope.
Look up high to see the gleaming green dome
The mosaics inside will remind you of Rome.

15

This home's place in history has long been cemented
As the place where the cocktail party was invented.
The family moved on in 1924
And sold to the church that is almost next door.

_____

_____

16

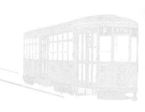

If you find you're deep in contemplation
Head straight to this sacred location.
Two temples and three churches, you'll find
Located along an old streetcar line.

_____

_____

17

Abode to a playwright—a prolific fellah—
Whose most famous line is probably "Stella!"
He moved to St. Louis when he was eight
But shares his name with a nearby state.

_____

_____

18

Find on a Founding Father's street
A chef's food homage to historic elite.
Haute cuisine brings smiles to every face—
Bustling bar and seating in a very large space.

_____

_____

19

Once home to those listed in society's blue pages
The nickname would fit well on *Sesame Street* stages.
Each section reflected a Boston pedigree
If you want to remodel, neighbors must agree.

20

He started out life as just plain Tom
Living here with his dad and mom,
Sharing space with W., T. S., and K.,
Perched near the bookstore window bay.

1

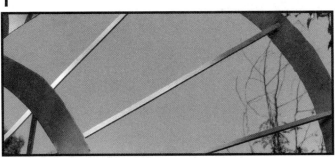

Named after a mayor from the last century,
Check out the paths through the lush greenery.
As you wander slowly exploring the grounds
Colorful artwork serenely surrounds.

2

A mighty fortress comes to mind
Its tower crowned by a cross divine.
The old crowing weathervane hides inside
Deep within this place's archives.

3

Named for the last car on the train tracks
To see two at once might take you aback.
Lovingly restored, these cars have survived
To honor the trades that made the city thrive.

4

If you make smoothies in your blender
Check out the produce from this spot's vendors.
May through October they give you a reason
To taste the flavors of the autumn season.

5

This youth sits with a stack he picked
In this public place—an American classic.
You can tell this is surely the place to be
Where knowledge is given to all for free.

6

Named for the first Christian martyr
Its markets open to barter.
You're sure to sing praises loud and be vocal
When you discover products both fresh and local.

7

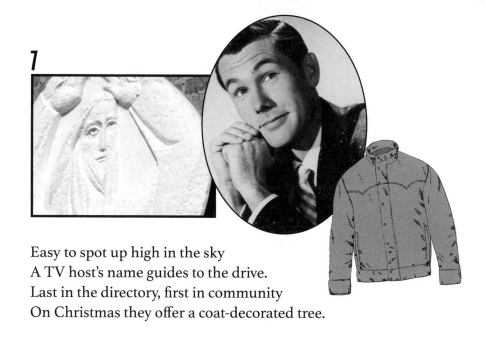

Easy to spot up high in the sky
A TV host's name guides to the drive.
Last in the directory, first in community
On Christmas they offer a coat-decorated tree.

_____

_____

8

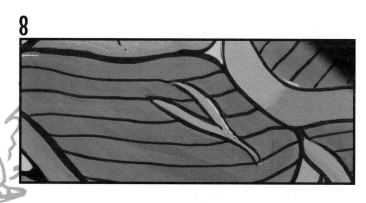

His prime location is behind the original—
Inside are prime cuts and sides irresistible.
Loyal customers even helped move the food
Keeping everyone working and in a good mood.

_____

_____

9

Find the building that's the new hub
For this amazing and historic youth club.
Gardening, yoga, robotics, and more
For neighborhood teens to learn and explore.

10

Keep your eyes peeled as you walk
You might miss it if you stop to talk.
Pretend you are playing I Spy—
Find the best local place for pie.

11

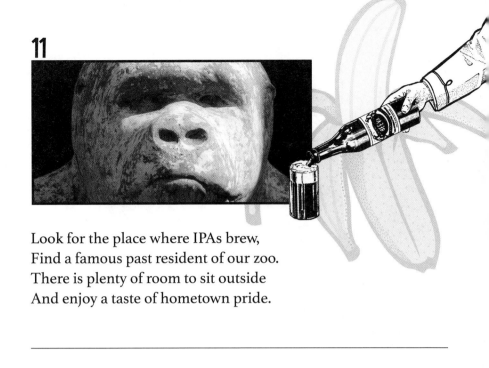

Look for the place where IPAs brew,
Find a famous past resident of our zoo.
There is plenty of room to sit outside
And enjoy a taste of hometown pride.

_____

_____

12

The name would lead you to look down
But the site is quite high above town.
A horseshoe appears for one-way traffic—
Take a class here and design a graphic.

_____

_____

13

Named after the recently canonized mother,
Stories in the windows stun like no other.
The new location creates quite a vision
India was where she carried out her mission.

14

In a park named for two new beginnings
It's a great place to spend the day fishing.
The second part of the name is no trouble at all
If you just think of that famous "Cannonball."

15

Almost the same name as the park in the city
You can play a match that gets nitty-gritty.
If you decide handball isn't your thing,
The tennis court will make you feel like King.

16

If you're looking for a place for a klatch or a class
You probably want to get here fast.
You can even host a private celebration
By simply making a reasonable donation.

17

This park shares the name of a famous bay
And is a wonderful place to stop and play
A round of golf or enjoy a stroll—
Beauty abounds near the 18th hole.

_____

_____

18

Although TLC said these shouldn't be chased
This area is quite a magnificent place.
Follow the path and go the full distance,
Discover a new home for your business.

_____

_____

19

Getting here is just the start
Of a 392-foot tunnel of art;
Fun for kids and adults alike
When you take a trip on your bike.

20

NATIONAL REGISTER
OF HISTORIC PLACES
1895

Built on this street at the turn of the century
The locations are now bound to the scenery.
One, two, and three stories tall
On the National Register you will find them all.

1

A writer believed slavery wasn't right
His offices vandalized in dark of night.
Pro-slavers tossed his printing presses in the river—twice!
Thrice attacked, he paid the ultimate price.

2

"Come on down!" where water falls and rises
Safely guiding boats of all shapes and sizes.
Eight stories up offers a bird's eye view;
Go in the winter to see eagles, too!

3

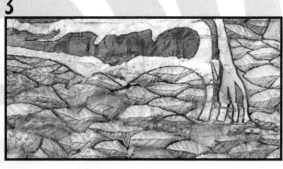

Am I a bird? A dragon? No, neither.
I'm an Illini mythological creature.
Once destroyed was the first petroglyph
But immortalized again on the cliff!

_____

_____

4

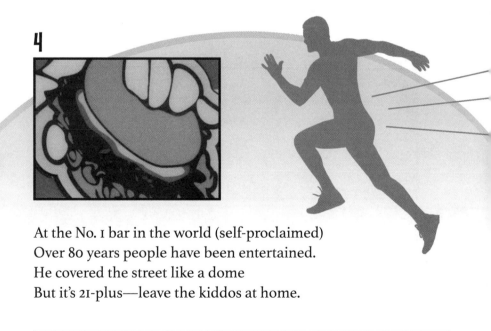

At the No. 1 bar in the world (self-proclaimed)
Over 80 years people have been entertained.
He covered the street like a dome
But it's 21-plus—leave the kiddos at home.

_____

_____

5

Maybe that sound was clucking you heard;
This drive-in is famous for its giant bird
Decked out in a tux and hat but no cane—
The food is so good, you'll be back again!

6

Designed by the architect of St. Louis Station,
The stained glass windows have no imitation.
The congregation first, though the building third—
With luck today, the pipe organ may be heard!

7

I look akin to a castle of stone.
Eliot—my founder—a preacher well-known
Not just by locals who pray there the most
But also those seeking the hanged pastor's ghost.

_____

_____

8

For over a century, I have stood strong,
Welcoming guests with theatre and song.
I've been made new after years of rejection
You can see my name from any direction.

_____

_____

9

Life-size dollhouse built for Lucy's birthday—
It mirrored her home in every way.
Sadly she died and since it brought such joy
Mom gave it to share with others in Illinois.

10

History was made here in 1858—
Alton held this famous Senatorial debate.
Though Abe didn't win this statewide election
The country survived under his steadfast direction.

11

Some towns have a small welcome sign
But we have a bigger one by design!
With letters and a flag that are sky high
You can't help but smile as you drive by!

12

The "Birth of the Cool" was born here—
He played for Charlie Parker for years.
Inducted into the Rock & Roll Hall of Fame
But it was something Blue that won acclaim.

13

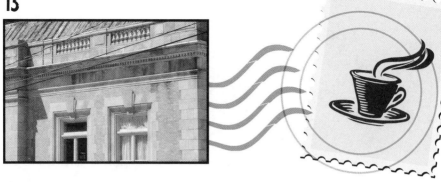

I once was home to mailboxes and letters
Yet now a place to gather together.
It's time for the coffee and brunch that you crave;
A work of art for all, I have been saved!

14

This unique building with a corner tower
Is as brightly painted as a blooming flower.
It started its life as a department store
Before it sold gowns to brides by the score!

15

Now we're getting to the point, as they say
Some cash their checks here on payday.
Need something stored under key and lock?
Just head to the door underneath the great clock.

TO BE,
OR NOT
TO BE.

16

Parties held at this locale were lavish
But a firm hold could not be established.
Named for the birthplace of The Bard
They are trying to save it, although it is hard!

17

I am what's left of the Forest Park fair
Hand-carved German wood, Wiseman built me with care.
Filled with portraits and a dance hall no more
Now I am home to a General Store.

_____

_____

18

Four husbands all alike went insane
Ms. Drummond sold me to a man of fame.
My bright yellow paint is something to see—
You can stay here, too; I'm now a B&B!

_____

_____

19

An Italianate structure three stories tall
Damaged in a fire, but the tower did not fall.
Lovingly restored in several phases
It's on the Register of Historic Places!

_____

_____

20

As there are rest stops along the highway
Migrating birds stop here on the flyway.
Named for a naturalist, world-renowned
The area's hidden gem lies just west of town.

_____

_____

1

A grand opening, 1921 was the year
Movietone Clips started playing here.
It sounds like the place you'd see the *Baldknobbers*,
Later films became plays with actors as robbers.

2

Take a class here if to the art of prayer you aspire
At the place with the striking gothic stone spires.
Started by Germans on the American Frontier
Ambassador and Mrs. Walker funded an institute here.

3

It may take some time to locate this structure
Though it has stopped roaming at this juncture.
Money made from the gun that settled the West
For a party, the Hearth Room is the best.

4

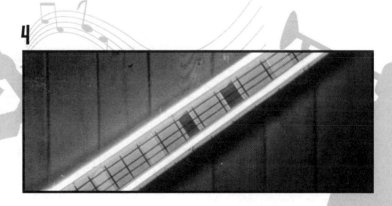

Bill says, "Laissez les bon temps rouler!"
As the Zydeco washboard player scratches away.
Look inside for the Mardi Gras Countdown Board
Drive down to the home of the Blues in your Ford.

5

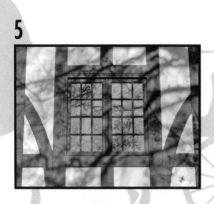

A garage before there were autos,
Houses local producers of shows
Making sure performers and directors are glad
Performing in the place named after Conrad.

_____

_____

6

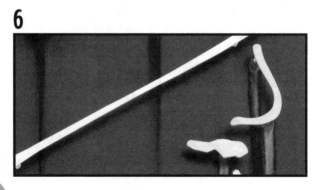

It sports the name of the sedan
Driven by Howard Cunningham.
For flambé and Cleopatra they are known
You are now looking at their third home.

_____

_____

7

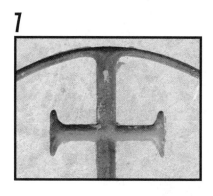

GO SHaRPieS!

With roots deep in the Bluegrass State
The order wanted to provide something great
Giving young women educational opportunity
Whose mascot is another word for Sharpie.

_____

_____

8

I love their offerings from my head TO-MA-TOES
I go green with envy when the broccoli shows.
Stop at the triangle on your way into town
Find out the latest farming lowdown.

_____

_____

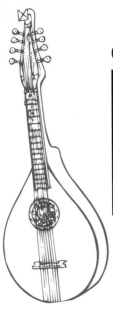

9

If Vince Gill inspires you to learn mandolin
These helpful people invite you to step in.
Learn a riff and a rhythm as you strum a banjo—
Keep practicing and you might get a standing O!

10

You know it can be a jungle out there—
But experts are waiting to help you in here.
They'll help you get prepped to explore like a pro
They have all you need, so get ready to go!

11

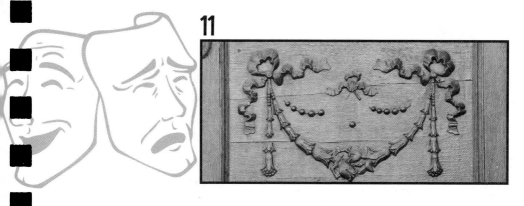

Fun and merriment await you here
In this place of community actors amateur.
Look and you will find the name in the lane.
If you audition, a role you may gain.

_____

_____

12

Owned by a rail fan club since 1994
Peek in the windows to see models galore.
You are looking for Baker on the BNSF line
Look close—if you're lucky, this treasure you'll find.

_____

_____

13

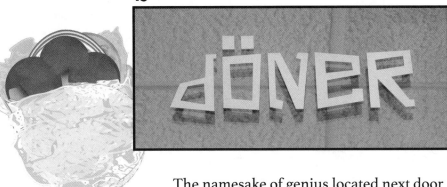

The namesake of genius located next door
East Europe's fine flavors all there to explore.
Authentic cevapi and somun to sample
From Loryn and Edo the "off'rings are ample."

14

Want to escape from the continent today?
Find the place with a griffin proudly displayed.
Have a pint or a rarebit or a savory pie—
Find many delicious Celtic dishes to try.

15

Once a feed company stable
Now you can buy farm-to-table.
Look for a sign of green and white
Buy seeds, plants, and even an epiphyte.

16

What's this mess on my shirt? It was practically new!
Come see the miraculous things they can do;
They will take out that spot. Bid it adieu!
Tired of ironing? They'll press clothes for you!

17

It could be named for a decimal system—
Find exotic toppings, if that is your mission.
A new cook in the kitchen will be impressed
As unusual ingredients are used with finesse.

18

Is it named for a street or the ancient prover?
Step inside! You may find you're a mover and groover.
Rockers may find "25 or 6 to 4,"
For punkers Sid & Nancy will be their score.

19

1892

Horses awaited a farrier's aid
(Good thing they were trained in the blacksmithing trade!)
Owned by the man whose first name means dollar
His surname is something you might chop up in a holler.

20

Rail passengers waited here for a ride to hire
The station name is the same as After Six attire.
The caretaker/owner did a great renovation—
Stop by, grab a bench, and admire the station.

1

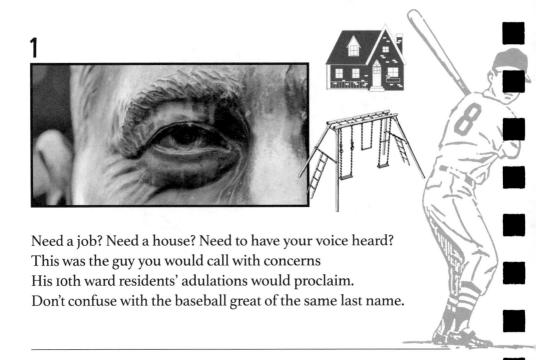

Need a job? Need a house? Need to have your voice heard?
This was the guy you would call with concerns
His 10th ward residents' adulations would proclaim.
Don't confuse with the baseball great of the same last name.

2

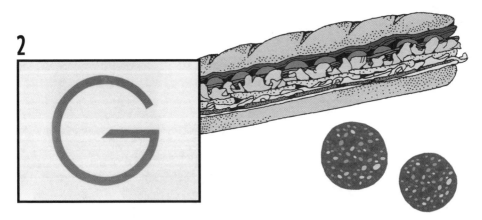

Known for the award from the James Beard Foundation
Their hot salami has a national reputation.
Happiness is another word for the name of this deli
And you will know what I mean when you fill your belly.

3

Look in the park for the blossoms and blooms
Volunteers made light work when they were given room.
From high up look down on the outline of the bed
And admire the map of the green, white, and red.

_____

_____

4

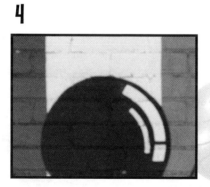

A place to throw a "boccin" or "pallino"
While sipping on a glass of vino.
Upstairs you will find the local realtor
Of your housing needs she takes "bene" care.

_____

_____

5

Named for a patron of keepers of bees,
The bell's toll from the tower is certain to please.
Take a quick peek when the doors open wide
And see why the neighborhood swells with pride.

6

A mom and pop at the joint of two streets
First in the region to sell Boar's Head meat,
Italian favorites like luganega and salsiccia;
Stop for a sweet treat or pick up fresh pizza.

7

A gathering place in the heart of The Hill
With Old Country warmth that charms us still.
Play some chess or enjoy a Gelato di Riso
Relax on a bench with Café Dolce cappuccino.

_____

_____

8

This place is where five streets commingle
Found beneath a soaring eagle.
A film about the robbery in '58
Starred Steve McQueen, an acting great.

_____

_____

9

Let's meet for a cup of joe in the vault—
(If I'm late to work it's the quiche's fault.)
All of the roasting happens right here—
Enjoy a whiff of it if you're near.

_____

_____

10

Kitchen tools, coffee presses, knives of every style—
Look for the culinary gadgets as you go down the aisle.
Sharpening tools for chefs creates a business that is steady.
They'll even pick up and drop off as soon as they are ready.

_____

_____

11

Home of the window with the rose,
Many a suitor here has proposed.
The yellow section filled with many a table
Used to be the brewery's local stable.

12

Nestled cozily under the highway
A favorite is Wine Down Wednesday.
Book an overnight and browse the antiques,
Dine under the pergola—Bon Appetit!

13

They moved across the street in 1970
Choice baking, cooking, and prep aids aplenty.
Diane and her family find unusual treats:
Pastas, spices, and candies—such wonderful eats.

14

A vision of heaven from above
Watching over the street with love.
Across from a members-only club
Smiling on shoppers at this foodie hub.

15

No longer used as a filling station
The restored pumps are just for decoration.
The name sounds like a race-lap break
Don't speed by—stop in for a steak!

16

A totally new concept in St. Louis's music scene:
Bands can record before a crowd enjoying cuisine.
Named after the city's most storied Square
Paying homage to entertainers who once performed there.

17

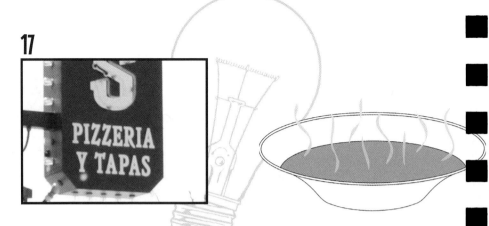

Look at the lights! Are we on Broadway?
Nope, we're on Shaw, not the Great White Way.
White bulbs spell out an Italian name
Yet delicious gazpacho is their claim to fame.

_____

_____

18

The place to come for authentic caponata
You may think you don't have time, but stop, you've just gotta!
Everything's made by the family with pizazz—
Tasty lunch fare, including the Mary and the Faz.

_____

_____

19

Locals remember coming here for the picture show
Lines around the block because everyone would go.
Lastly a racquet club 'til a fire burned it down.
The artistic owner shares his works with the town.

_____

_____

20

The windows displayed many a wedding cake
The Gambaro family would carefully bake.
Today the window display is no more
But there's still a great smell when you enter the door.

_____

_____

21

Mangia Bene

Find farm-to-table by Chef Anthony
His produce enhances any recipe!
Dine on the patio and enjoy a martini
When the evening is done you will say "Mangia bene."

22

By any other name
This place is still the same.
For your private dining and dancing event
Book a crowd for a wonderful night well spent.

23

Named after a self-made millionaire
Reading and writing happens there.
Continuing along with the nature theme
Plantings by its young artists are often seen.

_____

_____

24

Look for the cherubs hanging about
In front of a place you go to check out.
Sometimes you will see a faux rainfall
Drawing birds for a social call.

_____

_____

25

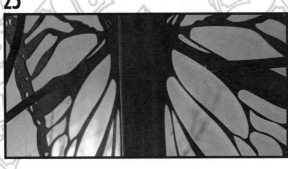

Across from the place that's a lender
A small space displays nature's splendor.
England's Queen and the King of Spain
Both share this insect's proper name.

26

While along this slanted street you dash
Check out this building's colorful splash.
Creative artists publish many a graphic
Even near all the rambling railroad traffic.

27

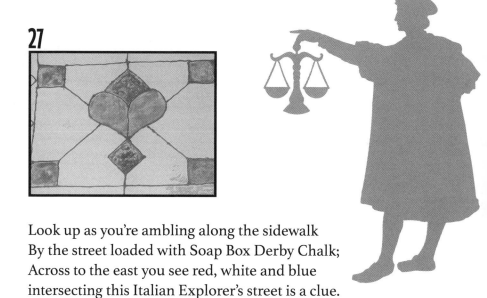

Look up as you're ambling along the sidewalk
By the street loaded with Soap Box Derby Chalk;
Across to the east you see red, white and blue
intersecting this Italian Explorer's street is a clue.

28

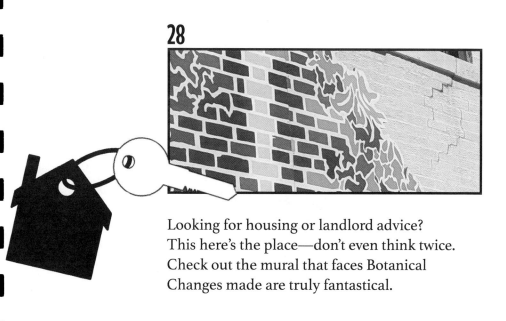

Looking for housing or landlord advice?
This here's the place—don't even think twice.
Check out the mural that faces Botanical
Changes made are truly fantastical.

1

His neighbor's building was shabby and sad
But Bob Cassilly didn't get crabby or mad;
He decided to put up a tale-telling frieze
Right on Washington Ave. for all to see.

2

Back in the day when hats were the thing,
This building's wares were fit for a king
With ads for a product that certainly was
Setting satisfied St. Louis patrons a-buzz.

3

When walking down Tucker, take a glance
You might think you're in Paris, France,
Watching folks pay their taxes and bills
In a replica of the old Hotel DeVille!

4

When the Supreme Court heard his petition
It became one of their most famous decisions.
Taylor Blow's enslaved clients are freedom icons
Forever immortalized near the Arch in Bronze.

5

If you look at the bottom of the beacon,
You'll see a Roman Goddess peeking.
As her torch enlightens faces
Of those deciding legal cases.

6

The flagship store of this celebrated group
Is still well-known for its beloved soup.
The "and" in the middle was finally dropped—
For years it remained the only place to shop!

7

Although this might sound a bit funny
At this museum they give you free money.
Of course, its torn up like confetti
Come and learn about markets aplenty.

8

Balconies that north and south, east and west look;
A palatial estate name and title of a book.
From the rooftop you can watch fireworks from the Fair
Or stand where George Clooney filmed *Up In The Air*.

9

Along the "zipper" old is new and new is old
Decorated with machines from workers untold.
Housing named after the German translation
Of the tallest man-made monument in our nation.

10

Two titans fight in a duel
Engaged in battle most cruel
Daily in combat they are locked—
Hmm, maybe I should check my stocks.

11

This building might seem kind of small
But 10 stories was once thought quite tall.
This early skyscraper in the nation
Shares a name with a pitching sensation.

12

Built for that famous World's Fair,
Twice hosted Democrat fanfare.
There is currently not one resident
In this building named for a president.

13

The man who wrote "Little Boy Blue"
Grew up in this house, it's true!
Now a museum that's full of old toys
That brought children of yore many a joy.

_____

_____

14

Named after a Governor of Missouri
St. Louisans here serve on a jury.
The columns will give it away
They're impressive even today.

_____

_____

15

Hurry along Market and don't tarry,
Find the site of the West's first library.
In '89 Director Hoover moved the collection
To a nearby university for archival protection.

16

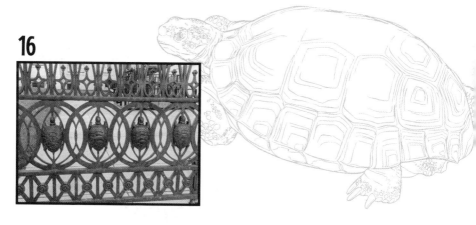

When passing the first place of law you might sense
Something peculiar 'bout that old iron fence.
If you pay heed and look quite close to the ground
You'll see replicas of Quigley's turtle abound.

17

If you are summoned here, don't dally
Fifth tallest building by my tally.
Named for a former politician
And inside, justice is the mission.

18

Thirsty patrons during Prohibition looked for the Blind Pig.
Others referred to it as a Blind Tiger, you dig?
Skip the red carpet and head round the back
Of this building that once was built for Kodak.

19

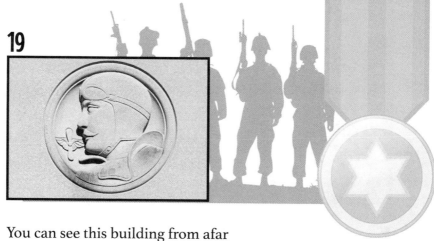

You can see this building from afar
Supported by wives and mothers Gold Star.
On a city block this building stands quietly and proudly
Having received much support from Gold Star Families.

20

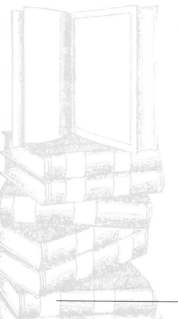

Look closely and see the faces and names
Of many writers who have garnered fame.
Looking for books, or movies, free rental?
Then this place is definitely fun central!

21

The first group, not Pope followers
Built near the house for borrowers.
Housing one of the top organs in town
Invites guests to listen from all around.

22

Statues of Mississippi and of Mo
Symbolizing how the rivers flow.
Across the street from this meeting place
Link designed and full of grace.

23

Buildings that held both garment and shoe
Reborn a destination avenue.
This popular thoroughfare is quite chipper
And this invention makes getting dressed quicker.

_____

_____

24

On the corner of this President's street
Once had ready to wear from head to feet;
Brown with letters in leaves of gold
Hints at models in outfits bold.

_____

_____

25

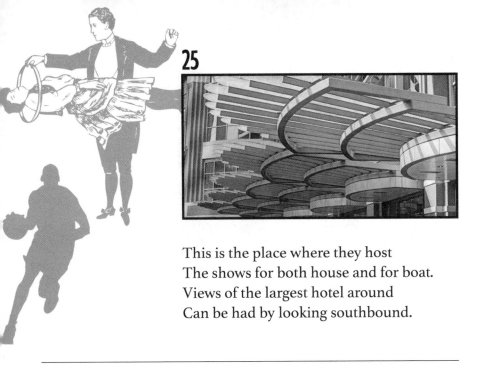

This is the place where they host
The shows for both house and for boat.
Views of the largest hotel around
Can be had by looking southbound.

26

Pop the cork at a celebration
Ten blocks northeast of Union Station.
Family and friends party the night away
Behind panes of glass dancers glide and sway.

27

This building is so very old
The property has never sold!
The roof was once faded to green
But now has a new copper gleam!

28

A monument known for its elevation
Come see the magnificent renovation.
Everything is so shiny and new
Even windows with a city view!

1

The sign might say old but the sinkers are new—
They are so good, there's usually a queue!
Powdered, frosted, plain, or with sprinkles
Just one bite and your eyes will twinkle.

_____

_____

2

Sharing the name of a king or a bull
This shrine once was completely full.
Home to the only saint from this region
Her devotion serves as a hopeful beacon.

_____

_____

3

With only two owners in 15 decades
Enjoy smells of delicious foods just made.
While patrons enjoy the award-winning offerings
A gentleman may kneel and offer his true love a ring.

4

Although its name means home in Spanish
It was built before the French claim vanished.
Second name is also a town in the Beaver State
This last link to Spain rescued before it was too late.

5

THIS IS THE INTERNATIONAL SPIRIT OF R(

ROTARY INTERNATIONAL

FLORISSANT ROTARY (
2000

Home to the town's first church made of logs
Now a park where you can run your dogs.
A long time ago the town was deeded the plot
But now there's no marker to show each grave's spot.

6

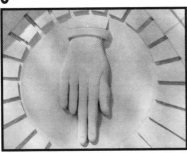

Blessed by the Belgian-born explorer
Who saw the future for the German poor.
You will spy the holy book over the door
Christ's spirit lends to welcoming more.

7

Although this home wasn't built by Dan Boone
It's similar to one that he would have hewn.
It's amazing today this structure still stands
In a royally named place on its original plot of land!

8

Franz heeded the call of California's gold rush
When he returned to his home, he was flush!
In land he decided promptly to invest
Here historians share the story without rest.

9

The name of this park is a liquid
And not only that, it means frigid!
Meaning a space where everyone shares the land
You might hear a song coming from the bandstand.

10

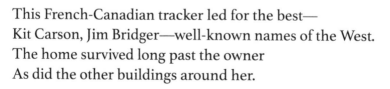

This French-Canadian tracker led for the best—
Kit Carson, Jim Bridger—well-known names of the West.
The home survived long past the owner
As did the other buildings around her.

11

Madame Chouteau's ox cart driver who lived to 110
Sold the property to Michael from Ireland—
Shaved buckskins and cash did he want
Michael's son became Mayor of Florissant!

_____

_____

12

When man's best friend passes and is buried
They can be interred in this cemetery.
Its name is both royal and regal
A fitting last rest for your kitty or beagle.

_____

_____

13

Wells saw the future of travel to the city and around
One hour was the ride for those St. Louis-bound.
Street cars took over, this building avoided demolition
It was saved by rail fans and moved to this location.

14

Over a century ago non-followers of the Pope
Together built a multi-denominational place of hope.
Although you no longer hear preaching on Sunday
It can be opened for those celebrating a special day.

15

Search for a red awning and lines to the street
Awaiting a brown cow or another treat.
An "Ultimate" means you ordered an upgrade
Take the first bite and you'll be glad you paid.

16

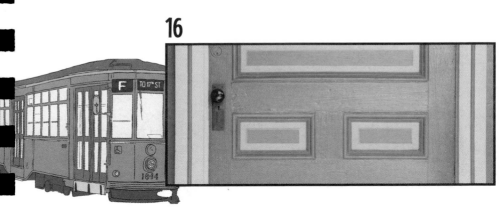

Initially the home took up a whole block
A family bought it one summer—lock and stock.
Back then St. Louis's air was heavily polluted
Dad rode the streetcar and daily commuted.

17

A French-style farmhouse with a sloping roof
Saved by a builder to have architectural proof.
The house is named for this man of the hour
Inside volunteers plan for Valley of the Flowers.

18

Ancestors wet their whistle after riding on the rails
Back then they carried beer out in buckets and pails.
Look for the green door not quite the color of lime
This century-old business changed names only one time.

19

Owned by Rita, an All-American Girls League player
A French-style log cabin at its deepest layer.
Find the street named after Buster of a local shoe company
And the saint of our city crowned at 13 and born in Poissy.

_____

_____

20

A famous Prussian cabinetmaker migrated to the city
His beautiful woodworking made St. Louis homes look pretty.
His son took a different route owning a creamery and a cannery
He built this home that resides on the national historic registry.

_____

_____

1

The gates of this historic park feature
A giant mythological creature.
You might see a reunion or marriage
Or ride in a horse-drawn carriage.

2

Perhaps St. Louis's most beautiful conservatory
Oft compared to Kensington Orangery.
Frogs hop from lily pad to lily pad outside
Frolicking around duck after duck as they glide.

3

While it looks like it is falling apart
These hotel remains are a work of art.
Once the victim of a great fire
The remains are piled to inspire.

4

Above your head appear
What some might call spheres.
A pedestrians-only south gate
Where three sidewalks conflate.

5

Painted on a clearing house for useful power
Perhaps it's a mosaic of a garden flower?
Students gaze from the west-facing window,
When school lets out, to the park they go.

_____

_____

6

Can you spy this structure so grand?
It's just perfect for hosting a band!
Henry always offered concerts on Sunday
Free for all to come and hear the music play.

_____

_____

7

If you like classical music you must
Stop by this German composer's bust.
His most famous work surely must be
"The Flight of the Valkyries."

_____

_____

8

Along the paths and over a stream
A bridge so bright, it actually gleams!
Under the arch crown is engraved
Each of the bridge builder's names.

_____

_____

9

Gently flowing, not with a gush
Built on a rookery looking lush;
In a mirror-like reflecting pool
Stop and enjoy this unique park jewel.

10

A wonderful place to take a break
Under the watchful eyes of firedrakes.
Design inspired by the Far East
A lovely place to have a special feast.

11

If you need a snack before supper
Why not stop in for a cuppa?
England's capital city was so admired
The building's name it did inspire.

_____

_____

12

A building trimmed in red, orange, and ecru
Where these five streets meet, here's a clue for two:
A type of screwdriver and military lingo for "I know"
Will get you to the streets where art is on show.

_____

_____

13

Handling collections of great fame
Opened in '27 to much acclaim.
Funded initially by the steel magnate
"Free and open" he did stipulate.

14

Born in a loft on Washington Ave
Was an idea for the most fun you can have—
Taking people's party pics
Using amphibian-esque optics.

15

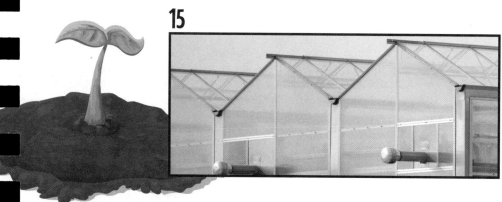

Glass greenhouses as far as you can see
Near to the park on the "Golden Arches" street.
MoBot is hopeful the seeds grow and succeed
Providing 95 percent of the garden's needs.

16

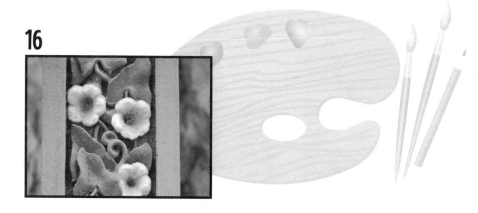

Art happens in this cozy cottage
Hoping to increase creative wattage—
Each day on adventures students embark
Around the neighborhood and throughout the park.

17

Baring teeth and flaring wings
Keeps away most evil things.
Find where the street named for the beehive state
Crosses the wood of which bourbon barrels are made.

_____

_____

18

In their second decade at this location,
This ad agency launched a transformation!
Need help with selling a product trademark?
Look for a church tower south of the park.

_____

_____

19

Across the street from Marti's triangular park
These city boys opened a fun hangout on a lark.
Successful and now a staple of Tower Grove South
Stop in and put some comfort food in your mouth.

20

The seven orders and laywomen's plan came to fruition
Lifting up girls to success through mindful education—
Above the entry stands the saint of young women
On the "Equality State" street find this school with a vision.

1

Name of a Broadway musical hit
Written by a country music wit.
They sell to all who are fitness-minded
Patrons bolt until their energy's grinded.

_____

_____

2

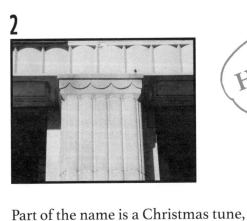

Part of the name is a Christmas tune,
Neighbors find their location's a boon,
Their columns are grand and awe-inspiring—
A good place to go with the wealth you're acquiring.

_____

_____

3

Mark your calendar for Sunday
Plan to enjoy a Bloody Mary.
Here you can also dine alfresco
Take a cake when home you go.

4

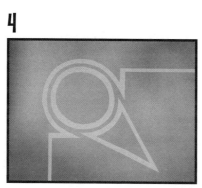

I scream, you scream, we all scream for vanilla bean!
Around the town their truck is often seen—
Naughty or Nice, choose from either list
And absolutely, positively NEVER a soft twist.

5

The place that started all the fun
Serves burgers on a brioche bun.
Walk in under the fedora all set
To meet with your friends for a hip tête-à-tête.

6

The boar is lucky in the Chinese Zodiac
Once you try the foods, you'll surely be back.
International dishes make you scream and shout
Dishes so tasty they'll make your waistband fill out.

7

A place with a beautiful steeple
An archway welcomes the people.
Back in the day, they even owned an alley
Where Dick Weber played and strikes he did tally.

8

High in the sky see the belltower square
For a century the congregation met there.
"Springs eternal" is frequently used with its name
Martin's followers often are called by the surname.

9

Founded the year The King rattled his last roll
Filling music into 10,000 square feet was the goal.
Wall-to-wall collections fill this old home of reading
Music lovers near and far keep them succeeding.

10

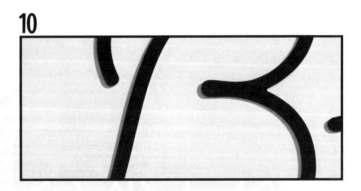

Only suds in small batches are offered here
No mega brands or large-quantity fare.
Learn from Cicerone-certified specialists
You'll go home with a brand new favorites list!

11

Named after Mamma and her progeny
Selling stuffed pasta and sauce to many.
Found on a street named after a cow
Visit to find Asian specialties now.

12

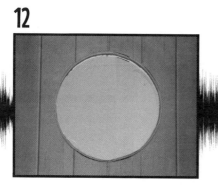

Not jagged, bitter, or hard to swallow,
This one is named after a primary color.
Commercials, podcasts, folk sessions, and rap,
Like all cool places, enter through the back.

13

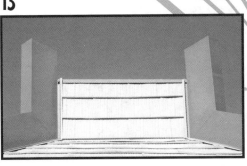

Waving from the top of the Arch with a smile
At the flying carpet holding Becky Queen of Tile.
Cooking dinner? Making Ice? Freezing a meal?
Visit these siblings and find out the deal.

14

Here request a refill, consultation, or delivery
Find the sign with the ancient name for pharmacy.
Cure a headache, a stomachache, or bad hair day—
Once you get here you'll feel better right away!

15

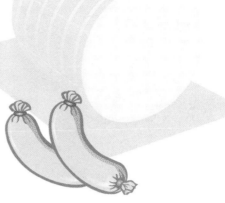

Much like the law, you just want the end product
Their sausage is delicious, their prices are modest,
The creations are tasty—secret family recipes
Try one and see if your taste buds agree!

16

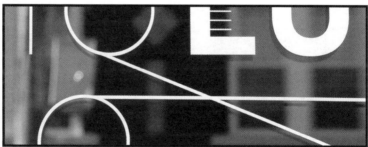

"Curl Up 'n Dye" faded out of style
But this name stands out along the Macklind Mile.
Look for this posh shop for all things tonsorial
You'll leave knowing you've been treated like a royal.

17

Happiness comes in a cup!
Order in or pick it up.
Let the Fox sisters start your day
Miles of smiles set you on your way.

18

A place for learning ABC's
Has been here over a century.
A German-born jeweler left a treasure
Planning her estate gift with good measure.

19

Survived a tornado and later the Depression
Near the old Sportsman's Park, its first location.
Considered a safe place to make your deposit
Dizzy Dean and Frank Frisch, too, took advantage of it.

20

The Presbyterians built this to educate
So children could learn and create.
Homes reside in the solid stone
An architectural serenity zone.

1

Look up for the sign, hopefully you can see,
The name of the oldest west of the Mississippi.
Only three years younger than the United States
Stop in and discover what amazing finds await.

_____

_____

2

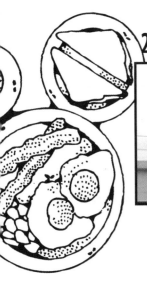

Late night, early morn, it just doesn't matter
Yum! Smell the griddle with pancake batter—
Corned beef hash or burgers and fries
They even have some amazing pies!

_____

_____

3

If it's early in the morning and you need a kick
Fresh coffee and a donut might do the trick.
His name's on the awning—a charming fellow—
Outstanding in bright red and yellow.

_____

_____

4

For 80 years this store has stood
With a variety of useful goods.
Stop in and buy the perfect gift for any age
It's the winner's choice, a Surprise Package!

_____

_____

5

A great place to stop in after your shift
Or whenever a pint you want to lift.
For live entertainment, check out the band
They might even be from Ireland!

_____

_____

6

Built as the worshipping community started to grow
This church was damaged by the Great Cyclone.
These Germans stayed and persevered
Clothing and feeding others happens here.

_____

_____

7

From its name, you might expect a friar,
But it's actually a venue you can hire.
The perfect place for weddings or celebrations
For you to invite friends and relations.

_____

_____

8

If it's BBQ that you dig,
Just look for the sign with the pig.
Located right there on the corner
Smell smoke? You know you're warmer!

_____

_____

9

Although it might look like a body shop or garage
It's a great place to eat with your entourage.
Brought to St. Louis by two brothers from Cali
If you like Mexican, it's right up your alley!

10

Follow the scent of hops and yeast
This playful fellow enjoys a feast.
Look up high and not down low
A stein of bevo he does hold.

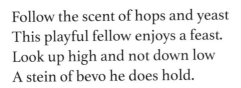

11

The structure stands tall and alone
Its first name engraved in stone.
Funded by Carnegie to help erase ignorance
The idea is reflected in the height of the entrance.

_____

_____

12

If you're looking for something in bloom
Simply have a walk around this room.
In Ireland this name is synonymous with luck
They'll even deliver your flowers by truck!

_____

_____

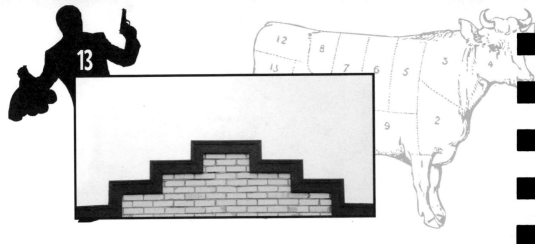

A Bohemian immigrant made his fortune in meat
Then groceries for the neighborhood to eat.
Surviving an armed robbery by James Earl Ray
The third generation is back in the city to stay.

Founded in the year of cholera and coal
Helping and healing was the parish's goal.
The gothic spires over the neighborhood soar
This corner location was restored in '84.

15

The smallest park is easy to miss
But it's a fine place to reminisce.
Just north of the brewery, this you can tell
Whenever they're brewing the barley you'll smell.

_____

_____

16

If there's a game you've wanted to play
Head over to this bar and café.
Tabletop, dice, card games and more,
The staff helps you navigate and explore.

_____

_____

17

After hitting the market, why not relax
And have a coffee amongst the stacks?
With amazing food and shelves 27 feet tall
Over 3,000 books—you'll never read them all!

18

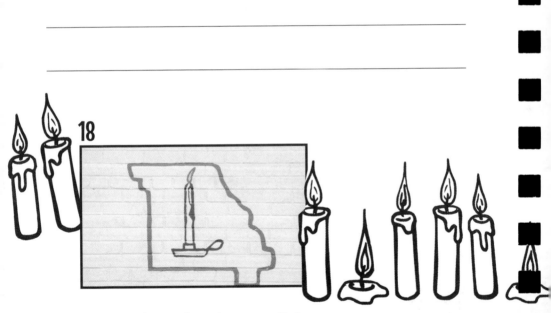

After the flames have been snuffed
What are you supposed to do with the stuff?
This place will recycle the remains
And soon you will be lighting again!

19

Want some drinks and eats with a NOLA flair?
Food delicious and beyond compare?
Now filling an acre after expansion
Ride their shuttle to catch the Cards in action.

20

Named for the chief of the Ottawa
This little park will fill you with awe—
The benches here are one of a kind
Looking like a massive feline!

1

Travel on the road to this shop
Create your own custom hat or top.
Neat finds on both shelf and rack
Its name could describe Jack Kerouac.

_____

_____

2

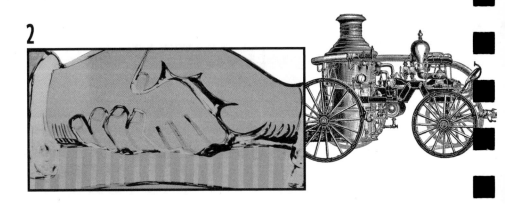

A historic building near town square
A gem of which most aren't aware.
See a famous steam engine named Jumbo
Look for a smithy shop brought from Chicago.

_____

_____

3

Name's the same as the home of the Pope
For over 150 years it's given people hope.
Patterned after Exeter Cathedral in England
It was built the year after the Civil War ended.

4

Find the studio where art meets light
He restored windows of F.L. Wright.
His stained glass is beyond compare,
He also creates pottery and dishware!

5

In the 1920s if you saw a show here
You might see Miss Rogers and Mr. Astaire.
Come in today for a new release movie
The pipe organ might play and she's a beauty.

6

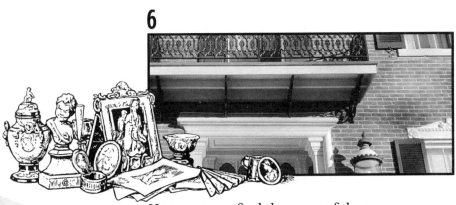

Here you can find the roots of the town—
A volunteer archivist can show you around.
A treasure trove housed in an old Victorian
You will go home a local historian!

7

A saloon built to sell Stag beer
Sadly closed for many a year.
Eventually after restoring and renewing
It's a monument to Belleville brewing.

8

Just hop in the car and go for a spin
They will direct you to a spot to pull in.
Kids under 12 get in for free
Tune to their dedicated FM frequency.

9

Before you send out an invitation
Check out their funky event location.
Home to galleries, parties, and concerts galore
Their name is what everyone goes there for.

10

You'll have to look carefully to find
Where the historic neighborhoods combine;
Less an intersection than a bend in the road
One street name is the inventor of the steamboat.

11

Head right this way, to the center of town
But watch out for those who are traveling around.
Flowing water can be observed
Where the area honors those who served.

12

Preserved as a foundation in excellent condition
This 1830s structure escaped demolition.
Inside a coal stove with bucket and shovel
We're fortunate this place was not turned into rubble!

13

Some people moved here for the historical places
Or running a B&B with smiles on their faces.
They are not too far from the old saloon
Where sadly there's no beer to consume.

14

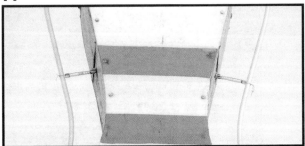

Set them up and knock 'em down
It's guaranteed to cure your frown.
You don't have to be the Fresh Prince
Just watch your fingers—don't get pinched!

15

Here a group of directors guide young learning
In an office where before letters were returning.
Look up and see a predator that can soar
Lurking over the entrance door.

_____

_____

16

Set next to a place named for a clock in London
It's filled with supplies and crafts in abundance.
Look for the awning with two colors of our flag
And you'll have this clue right in the bag.

_____

_____

17

Are you thirsty and want a local brew?
Boy, do I have some good news for you!
Grab a bite in the restaurant or just a drink
And watch the canning machine work in sync!

18

You might not remember *Leave It to Beaver*
But this place shows the designs of the Cleavers.
Restored as it was in 1952—
Even the kitchen's authentic to the period, too!

19

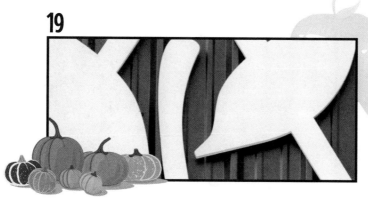

A local tradition for generations
Gather up your friends and relations.
They've done the hard work, now it's grown
You can go out to pick your own!

20

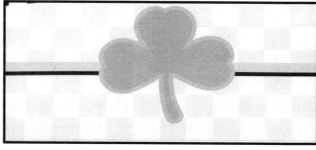

His dream plan is his dream pub
With plenty of beers and even some grub.
The décor is simple and green is its style
A leprechaun sits above the bar with a smile!

1

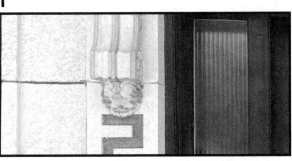

Looking to shine your pearly whites?
Stop in this place, they'll come out bright.
Near a mermaid and a steed
They can fill your every need.

2

Off the main drag, tucked in the neighborhood
Is a slice of history, surrounded by wood.
This one-acre park is worth a quick look
With a Little Library—check out a book!

3

Even though around us the city has grown
We're lucky they've saved this historic home.
The original owner's name is now a famous street
Since the land was donated for the new county seat!

_____

_____

4

The name in English translates to brothers
A perfect place to meet up with others.
Zoë transformed the old cobbler shop
Escargot for soles—she made a good swap!

_____

_____

Bon Appétit

5

It's easy to take some things for granite
But not when you're looking at the planet!
The students here will never be bored
With the entire world at their door.

6

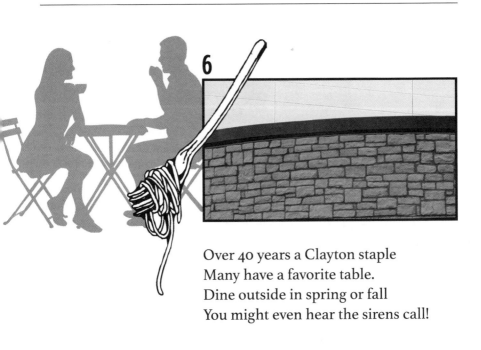

Over 40 years a Clayton staple
Many have a favorite table.
Dine outside in spring or fall
You might even hear the sirens call!

7

A Baptist Church started in this space
Then the Journey took over the place.
A synagogue north wanted to move south
The pastor and the rabbi worked a swap out.

8

Come see this building's brand-new face lift
Welcoming those who pair knowledge and thrift.
But don't bring in your soda or snacks
There's no food allowed when browsing the stacks.

9

When you're up so high it's easy to be vain.
But so few people look, isn't it a shame?
This rooster's home is where the city workers go.
He changes direction when the wind blows.

_____

_____

10

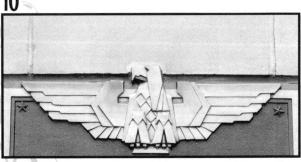

Over 100 years ago these brave men fought
Yet their sacrifice shall never be forgot.
Today this memorial continues to stand
See all the names carved on it by hand.

_____

_____

11

To find the place surrounded by scrolls
Head to a place to get a steamed roll!
You'll know that your journey is done
At the sign that says "Est 1881."

12

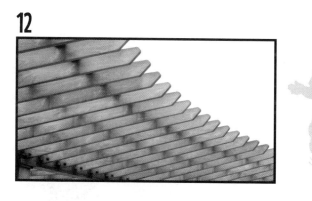

This recently constructed feature forms the basis
Of Clayton's newest renovated oasis.
A great place for the kids to run and play
While Moms and Dads appreciate the shade.

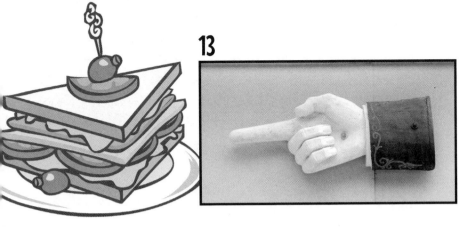

13

If there's a rumbling in your belly
Why not visit this historic deli?
You'll be happy that you came
To the place with the rhyming name.

_____

_____

14

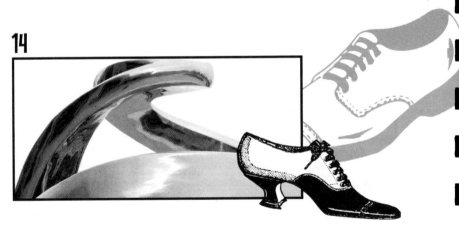

The name of this company was once Brown
But they're still the biggest shoe store in town!
Their new name is Latin and means "to glow"
In front of the building stands the new logo.

_____

_____

15

Between U-City and Clayton is a park you might like
With a wonderful trail that's fun for a hike.
You might have seen it from the highway above
It even has a waterfall—what's not to love?

_____

_____

16

This name is heard as a noun
That's used when people go out on the town.
A top hat and cane is the usual visual
When describing the hotel of the discerning individual.

_____

_____

17

West of Forest Park, you might fall under the spells
Of the carillonneurs as they ring the bells.
The music they play is fine and airy
From this tower located at the seminary.

18

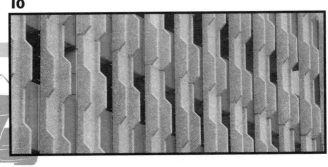

It looks like an office but looks can deceive
Instead it's a place to park your car for a fee;
The style is known as Brutalist form
But it will still protect your ride from a storm.

19

The most famous of fathers gives this place its name
In 1925 it was nearly destroyed by a flame—
Louis Gutman and others rebuilt it after the fire
And soon the spire was raised even higher!

20

You might think you're back on the British Isle
When you see this building in Tudor-style—
The dining room is such a wonderful venue
Full of "Lost Classics" as a part of the menu.

21

Founded in 1897 after a tragedy
This small town's disaster almost cost them their bakery
Only 20 years later, and they were all paid
And plans to protect high rises were laid.

22

A high-rise on the edge of a sphere
Wait . . . what is LIVESTOCK doing here?
Both a cow and a fish can be seen
Walk a block to the goat and pick up caffeine.

23

With the look of something that's from outer space.
Hunting for a davenport? This is your place.
You'll find it in Clayton, just south of the Moors
For over 30 years they've opened their doors!

_____

_____

24

The last one! Oh no, what a quandary.
Where do you go with dirty laundry?
They'll lift out stains like chocolate or red wine.
Even bring them your shoes, ready to shine!

_____

_____

1

Built with opera in mind
Now it's movies you will find.
The city got a grant to restore—
See comedy flicks, oldies, and more!

2

If you're looking for meat to chow
Just look for the Hereford cow.
A little slice of carnivore heaven
They've been here since 1947!

3

Three statues seen upon the steeple
Of this beautiful gathering place of people.
Always know the hour for prayer here
By the clock that is seen far and near.

_____

_____

4

They probably thought they were funny
Calling this bar a name that's quite punny!
You will know when you get here
When you see the name of a male deer.

_____

_____

5

If you wonder how you fill your cup
With water, well, just look up!
Built by a man with a heart for labor
Residents repaid him by working with fervor.

_____

_____

6

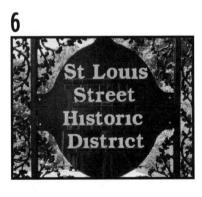

If you were rich in the old days and lived in town
This street was named for the city west and down.
All 51 addresses near this street
Have fascinating local histories complete.

_____

_____

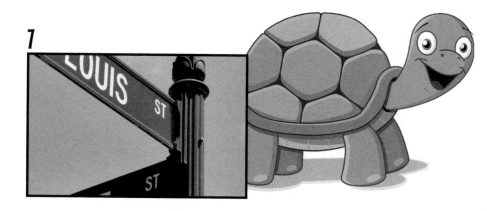

7

To get here you may have to jump a mental hurdle
And remember the name of Dr. Seuss's turtle.
Look for the crossed metal in black and white
You'll find this more easily in day than at night.

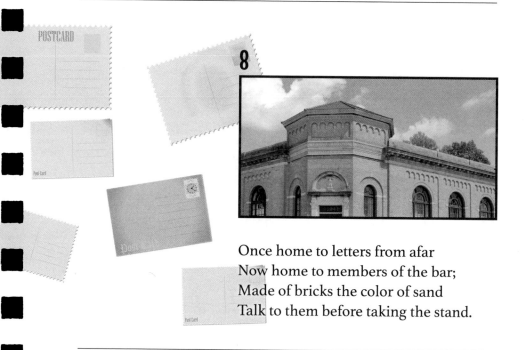

8

Once home to letters from afar
Now home to members of the bar;
Made of bricks the color of sand
Talk to them before taking the stand.

9

Restoring a building was their pursuit,
A former location for faith to take root
On a street named after a lover of the sunflower
Or the Illini rival who uses Rock Chalk power.

10

Was that Sally in the alley?
Perhaps she should be in a valley . . .
A replica of the work of FLW
A company in town can make one for you.

11

Thirty tons this behemoth weighs
Installed to celebrate a special day.
Moved to be visible to those who borrow
Media to be read at home tomorrow.

_____

_____

12

There once was a man who loved to roam
He wanted a piece to admire near home.
To his wife he gave a gift of water and air
So all could enjoy when visiting the city fair.

_____

_____

13

Built by a founder two centuries ago
He imagined how vital Edwardsville could grow;
Procuring from DC the public land sale office
Everyone buying property fell under its auspice.

14

Filled with preserved wetlands,
A lush place for amphibians.
Seek and find native species
Return visits are sure to please.

15

What started as a love of cake pops
Led this mom to open her own shop.
Pies and cookies abound, take a peek
They are open every day of the week!

_____

_____

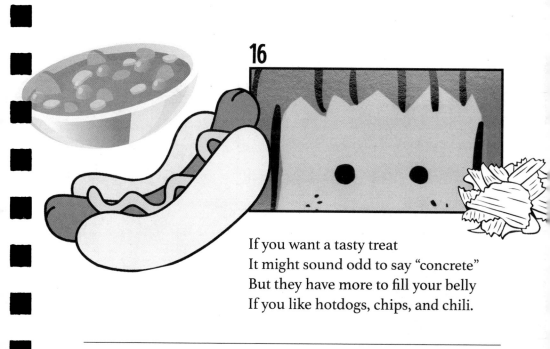

16

If you want a tasty treat
It might sound odd to say "concrete"
But they have more to fill your belly
If you like hotdogs, chips, and chili.

_____

_____

17

It might sound a bit strange to you
But the favorite here's a Horseshoe!
Whether for breakfast, lunch, or dinner
This local diner is surely a winner.

18

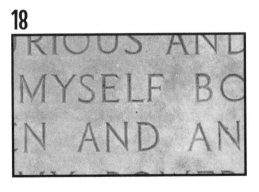

A secretary to the fourth President
Even though he was an Illinois resident,
He stopped the state pro-slavery legislature
Then freed his slaves and gave them 160 acres.

19

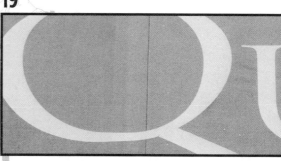

Love *The Crown* or *Downton Abbey*?
You must come here to enjoy high tea.
Complete with sweets and savories
The owner's known as the "Scone Lady."

20

Named after the break in school
This local brewery's real cool.
Matt learned his trade up in High Park
But came back home to make his mark.

1

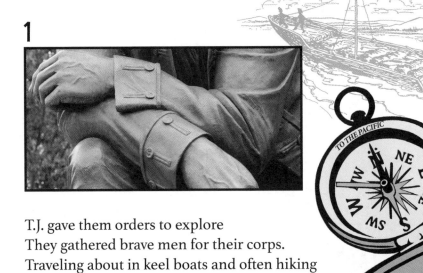

T.J. gave them orders to explore
They gathered brave men for their corps.
Traveling about in keel boats and often hiking
They mapped out the West to T.J.'s liking.

2

The legacy of the King of Spain
Lives on in the town's name.
Anglicized as a US city
Find it near the point of entry.

3

When people refer to it in conversation,
The spelling differs from pronunciation.
Santa comes here to have photos taken
And visitors pretend they're at a station.

_____

_____

4

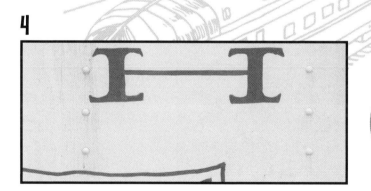

Hear the jingle, the rumble and roar along the line
From St. Louis to Detroit starting in '49.
You may have heard its name in an old folk song
With rhythm so driving, I bet you clapped along.

_____

_____

5

You can rent one built for two
Many choices are waiting for you;
Try one that has three wheels
In this riverside shop that also serves meals.

6

This historic place is known as a grist
The current supplied fuel and created a mist.
Stop by there now for a cold IPA
Perhaps a lager or pilsner will make your day?

7

You can spy it in the historic district from far away
The last stop before heading west to Santa Fe.
Check out the flora and the mural on the side
It's a popular place to visit for brides.

8

Wait, what's that amazing smell?
Create your own like casting a spell—
Bring it home in a jar for burning
To fill your house with the scent you've been yearning.

9

Starting a biz? Need to save your name?
Here's where people needing permits came.
Book lovers and browsers flock here in droves
Her reads make you happy from your head to your toes!

10

His niece married an abolitionist outspoken
A mob forced their household to be broken.
Her husband and uncle would be pleased to see
How this resident's business sets speech free.

11

Oh me, oh my, what is the time?
Stopping here doesn't cost you a dime
Relax on a bench in the beautiful grounds
Cross the street to where answers are found.

_____

_____

12

The first place of official postmarking—
Wishing against a stagecoach hijacking.
Then your money would be forever lost—
Today come here to be your own boss.

_____

_____

13

Find the heart of fun and entertainment
Under the iron painted the color of mint.
In the middle of shopping and historical markers
You may see a few people walking some barkers.

_____

_____

14

Cedar shake shingles atop it sit
The first place of state leadership!
Dedicated by the Knights of Columbus
Marking the location to forever remind us.

_____

_____

15

Tilt your head up and look closely
At art displaying flowers, mostly,
Between the place where men suit up
And another where you can drink and sup.

16

After dinner at Tony's stroll toward the Foundry,
Spy the place with the green glaze so shiny—
Look carefully, you'll see that the front is quite low
Now you can let the good times roll!

17

These unusual fellas met fraternally
Raising wealth to support local charity.
The balcony decor shows a tool of the trade
On which this Missouri River city was made.

_____

_____

18

The first duplex now here sits
Giving fodder to would-be wits
Saying the fearsome new family
Had made the groom uneasy!

_____

_____

19

Peacefully growing the state's heritage,
See these arching vines at a mature stage.
Absolutely no other region's foliage
Is allowed take root in this acreage.

20

Grab the patchouli, beads, and round sunnys
Crank up the Beatles—gee, that sounds funny!
Open the doors to take swinging photos
Enjoy a good vibe and rediscover your mojo.

1

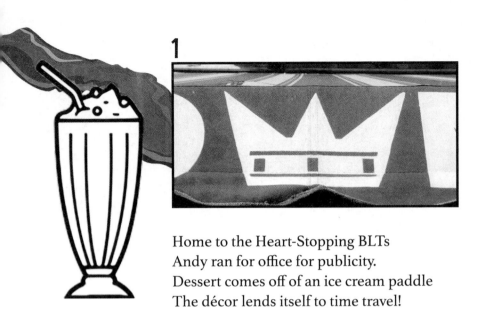

Home to the Heart-Stopping BLTs
Andy ran for office for publicity.
Dessert comes off of an ice cream paddle
The décor lends itself to time travel!

2

A triangle with a Little Library and trees
See the blocks that sit below your knees.
Named for a beloved volunteer and educator
She would be thrilled they named it for her.

3

The name includes the title of a famous opera
It attracts all sorts of members of the Lepidoptera.
Part of the name can mean setting your sight
If you're lucky you'll see the tenants take flight.

_____

_____

4

You can walk along the brick under the arbor
Named to remember the happiness Johnnie harbored.
Sitting on the bench or walking around
Pleasantries about the greenery abound.

_____

_____

5

Artists devise and create and perform
To collaborate here is always the norm.
A petal of gold color appears above the window
Often you may view a gallery show.

6

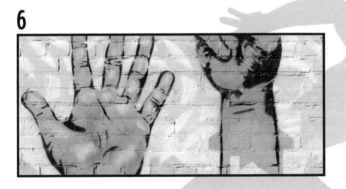

A winner known worldwide
For his incredible sprinter's stride
Breaking three world records in a row
Students painted he who couldn't go slow.

7

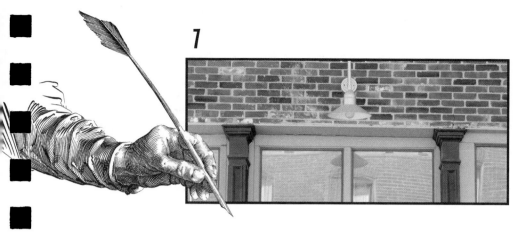

While teaching the children, MK had a vision:
He started a non-profit—that was his mission.
The very first project was a poetry lesson
Now they exhibit all artistic expression.

8

Though the name may be confused with that place in KC
The original name used the number of the street.
The logo on the building abbreviates pound
Look hard to see it—it's high off the ground.

9

Years ago you may have shopped for a dress
Today learn how to use a letterpress.
Experience Mark Twain's first profession
Make a birthday card or invitation.

10

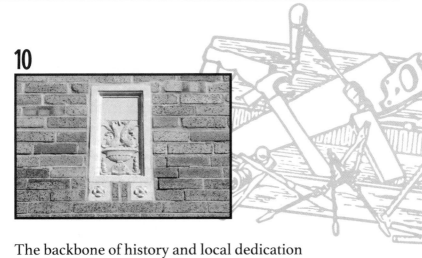

The backbone of history and local dedication
Organized to create a desirable destination.
Look for the building with cream-colored brick
Once you have found it that should do the trick!

Tilting at windmills gave him a thrill
Next door sells java that'll fit the bill.
Our favorite team's mascot perches
Next door you find pastries to purchase.

12

A circular plot drawn in 1916,
Deeded to the city was this site so serene.
Family and friends meet for picnics and fun
If it rains, don't worry, there's somewhere to run.

13

Black and white squares signal a match
Bring your own pieces to play on this patch.
Planning and skill you must coordinate
A powerful queen controls the king's fate.

14

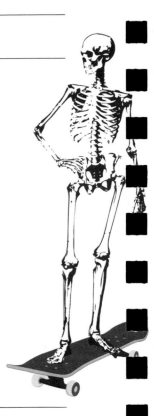

Named after the patron saint of good death
Skaters and bikers can scarce catch their breath!
Striving for mastery like Hawk and Landeros
Competitors like to run up ramps the most.

15

Stock up on your favorite delights
Microgreens grown right on sight.
Gather with friends at a table to dine
Enjoy great selections that all taste divine!

16

Originally named for an archangel
Then updated for a new flock of faithful.
Facing the highway on street number 11,
The building holds this great congregation.

17

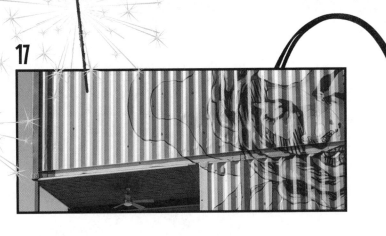

Don't panic, you're not in a shipyard—
Though this home may still catch you off guard
The deck boasts a nice view of the Arch.
The fair's fireworks might even rain sparks!

18

Groucho, Chico, Zeppo, and Harpo are brothers
Whose namesake store will have you covered.
Founded the year of the city's divorce
146 years later, they're staying the course.

19

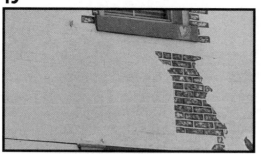

On the street named for Senator Thomas Hart
This painting is a remarkable display of art—
Along the top are birds at play
Find the shape of the Show-Me State.

20

Creators of eternal decorations
There reflects their great patience—
Fencing and railings and gates
Are some of the things they create.

1

Everyone makes a rush to the door
When they hear someone yell "All Aboard!"
If you see the round tower out back
Then you know you are on the right track.

_____

_____

2

Corinthian columns mark your arrival
To this historic Georgian Revival.
This is where the work gets done
To help the city of Kirkwood run!

_____

_____

3

High overhead three flags wave
Honoring those who were exceptionally brave;
Upon this memorial their names are recalled
Etched for all time upon this stone wall.

4

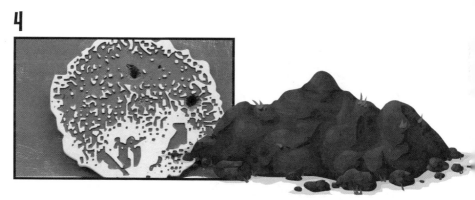

Owned by a politician with a name quite dirty
He divided the area all the way from Jeff City.
A historic structure built before the Civil War
This place is open for a special event or a tour.

5

Take a seat at the counter or booth
Grab a bite or indulge your sweet tooth.
They have a clock that won't let you be late
When waiting for that special date.

_____

_____

6

If you're looking to pick up some chicks
Or just the right grass seed mix,
Come in for great deals and bargains
On things for your henhouse and gardens.

_____

_____

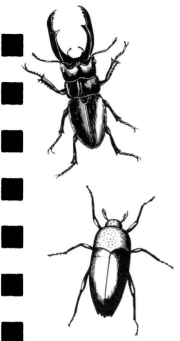

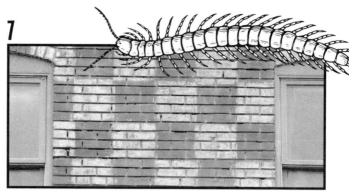

7

Initially they sold predator insects
To help keep out pesky garden pests.
Their stock hit the floor, they now sell décor
Find ornamentation for both in and outdoor!

_____

_____

8

SWEET

If you're craving something sweet
Then this store just can't be beat—
Products used to be made of dough
Now it's candy and goodies to go!

_____

_____

9

A place filled with wonder and learning
It will keep kiddos often returning.
So much there that's truly amazing
Like the Van de Graaff generator—it's hair-raising!

10

If you are looking for foods from afar
This shop should be on your home radar.
They sell meats, veggies, and various spices
From over 50 countries at incredible prices.

11

If you're a hockey fan, you're in luck
See your favorite team chase the puck.
After you hear the last penalty whistle blow
Call up a friend and now you take a go!

12

Actors come from all over the nation
To perform at their newest location.
So why not be part of the crowd
And applaud them as they take a bow?

13

Great deals must be the reason
The people come back every season
To find fresh food and produce
Or even apple cider and juice!

14

In a small building not far from the station
You can give in to a frozen temptation—
Get a sundae, a float, or concrete
And enjoy a local favorite treat.

15

Second location west of the river in 1853
The name includes a peaceful tree.
Today welcoming all from any location
Keeps this a thriving arm of the denomination.

16

If you love things that move
Of this location you'll approve—
They have Bobby Darin's car and over 70 trains
If you look around you'll see a couple of planes!

17

After achieving international fame
He opened this place under his own name.
Macarons, croissants, and pastry—
Why must everything look so tasty?

18

It sounds like your compagno's address
But it's an actual business nevertheless.
They are known for authentic cuisine
A great place to see and be seen!

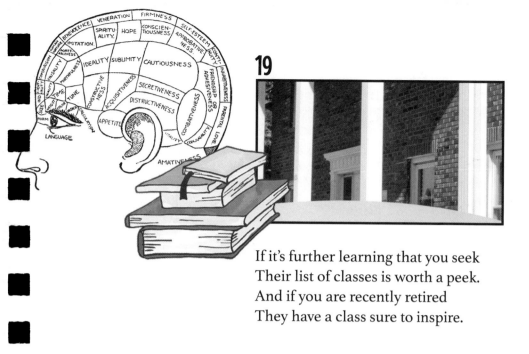

19

If it's further learning that you seek
Their list of classes is worth a peek.
And if you are recently retired
They have a class sure to inspire.

20

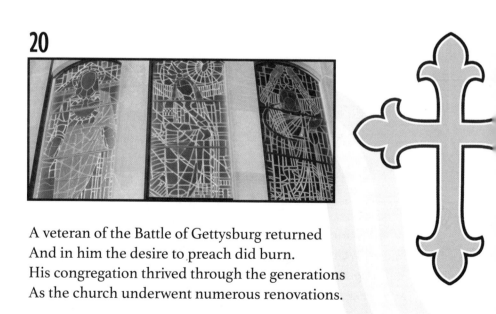

A veteran of the Battle of Gettysburg returned
And in him the desire to preach did burn.
His congregation thrived through the generations
As the church underwent numerous renovations.

21

If you are a fan of the Prairie Style
Seeing this structure will make you smile.
Designed by the movement's front runner
This small building is really a stunner!

_____

_____

22

Named not for the writer but his grandfather
Who took Universal ideals and spread them farther.
They also use his name for the newsletter, Greenleaves.
They welcome any and all under their eaves.

_____

_____